Kyle Wears a Smile

Mary Elizabeth Salzmann

Consulting Editor, Diane Craig, M.A./Reading Specialist

ABDO
Publishing Company

Published by ABDO Publishing Company, 4940 Viking Drive, Edina, Minnesota 55435.

Printed in the United States.

Credits
Edited by: Pam Price
Curriculum Coordinator: Nancy Tuminelly
Cover and Interior Design and Production: Mighty Media
Photo Credits: BananaStock Ltd., Brand X Pictures, Comstock, Digital Vision, Hemera, PhotoDisc, Rubberball Productions, Stockbyte

Library of Congress Cataloging-in-Publication Data

Salzmann, Mary Elizabeth, 1968-
    Kyle wears a smile / Mary Elizabeth Salzmann.
        p. cm. -- (Rhyme time)
    Includes index.
    ISBN 1-59197-800-9 (hardcover)
    ISBN 1-59197-906-4 (paperback)
    1. English language--Rhyme--Juvenile literature. I. Title. II. Rhyme time (ABDO Publishing Company)

PE1517.S354 2004
428.1'3--dc22
                                                                        2004047361

SandCastle™ books are created by a professional team of educators, reading specialists, and content developers around five essential components that include phonemic awareness, phonics, vocabulary, text comprehension, and fluency. All books are written, reviewed, and leveled for guided reading, early intervention reading, and Accelerated Reader® programs and designed for use in shared, guided, and independent reading and writing activities to support a balanced approach to literacy instruction.

Let Us Know

After reading the book, SandCastle would like you to tell us your stories about reading. What is your favorite page? Was there something hard that you needed help with? Share the ups and downs of learning to read. We want to hear from you! To get posted on the ABDO Publishing Company Web site, send us e-mail at:

sandcastle@abdopub.com

SandCastle Level: Fluent

Words that rhyme do not have to be spelled the same. These words rhyme with each other:

aisle

style

dial

tile

mile

trial

vial

pile

smile

while

Allen stretches his legs before running the **mile**.

At the grocery store, Kindra and her parents shop in every **aisle**.

Ted makes a big **pile** of sand at the beach.

Libby pushes the buttons to dial the phone.

When the girls play in the leaves, it makes them **smile**.

Gregory is having his hair cut in a new **style**.

Bob splashed soapy water on the tile walls.

Tessie did well at her gymnastics trial.

After school, the kids played for a little while.

When Sandra gets sick, her mom gives her medicine from a **vial**.

Kyle Wears a Smile

Kyle is on trial
because he always wears a smile.

In the courtroom,
people fill every aisle.

They want to hear
just what makes Kyle smile.

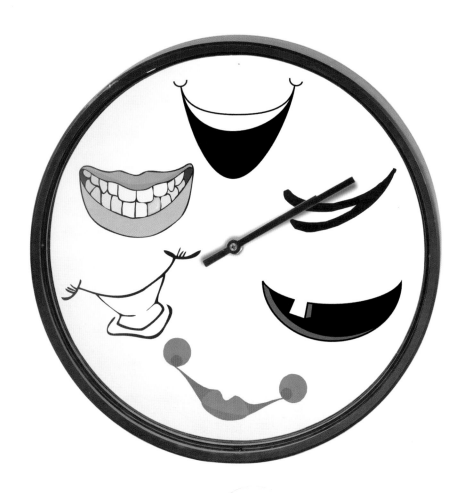

Kyle said, "I guess my smile
is just part of my style.

Every day I spin a dial
to find the right smile."

The judge asked, "But Kyle, what makes you smile?"

"Everything!" said Kyle.

"Even running a mile
while being chased
by a crocodile."

"But maybe it's dumb to always smile,"
said Kyle.

He put each smile in a vial
and threw them all in a pile.

He said, "I'll try wearing a frown for a while."

Upon seeing the frown on Kyle, the judge said, "Not guilty!" and closed the case file.

"Take back every vial and always wear a smile!"

Case: Kyle's Smile

Rhyming Riddle

What do you call the area in a store that sells clocks?

Dial aisle

Glossary

case. in the legal system, the facts and evidence offered to support a claim made in court

courtroom. a room where legal matters are discussed and trials are held

dial. to enter a phone number on a telephone; a device on which a measurement or selection, such as speed or a television channel, is indicated by a moving needle or pointer; the face of a clock

file. a collection of related papers and documents

tile. a piece of hard material, such as baked clay, concrete, or stone, that is used to cover walls, floors, or roofs

vial. a small, closeable container for liquids

About SandCastle™

A professional team of educators, reading specialists, and content developers created the SandCastle™ series to support young readers as they develop reading skills and strategies and increase their general knowledge. The SandCastle™ series has four levels that correspond to early literacy development in young children. The levels are provided to help teachers and parents select the appropriate books for young readers.

Emerging Readers
(no flags)

Beginning Readers
(1 flag)

Transitional Readers
(2 flags)

Fluent Readers
(3 flags)

These levels are meant only as a guide. All levels are subject to change.

To see a complete list of SandCastle™ books and other nonfiction titles from ABDO Publishing Company, visit www.abdopub.com or contact us at:
4940 Viking Drive, Edina, Minnesota 55435 • 1-800-800-1312 • fax: 1-952-831-1632